ThePeopleAlchemist Press is an imprint of The People Alchemist Ltd, a company founded by Laura Mariani, bestselling author of non-fiction success books for women and Change & Transformation Expert.

ThePeopleAlchemist Press publishes self-help, inspirational and transformational books, resources and products to help #TheWomanAlchemist in every woman/girl to change their life/career and transmute any circumstance into gold, a bit like magic to **Unlock Ignite Transform.**

ISBN: 978-1-915501-32-5

Books by Laura Mariani

STOP IT! It is all in your head

Think Look Act The Part Series
Think The Part - The Workbook
Look The Part - The Workbook
Act The Part - The Workbook

Unlock Ignite & Transform Your Career

90 Days To Reboot Your Career: How To Reinvent Yourself, Your Career and Your Life
90 Days To Reboot Your Career Planner: Career Plan Journal Notebook
90 Days Coloring Book: Relaxation Stress Relief and Empowerment for Women

Unlock Ignite & Transform Your Life

I don't care if you don't like me: I LOVE ME!: 28 Ways to Love Yourself More - a Self-love book with guided practices
28 Days To Love Yourself More - Planner and Guided Journal with Prompts for Women
28 Ways to Love Yourself More Coloring Book: Relaxation and stress relief for women

Shreem Brzee: **Making The Immaterial Material with the
Mantra for Wealth, Love and Happiness.**

Unlock Ignite & Transform Your Language Skills

Short Stories in English/Italian: Unlock Ignite & Transform
Your Language Skills with Contemporary Romance - Book 1
Short Stories in English/Italian: Unlock Ignite & Transform
Your Language Skills with Contemporary Romance - Book 2
Short Stories in English/Italian: Unlock Ignite & Transform
Your Language Skills with Contemporary Romance - Book 3
Short Stories in English/Italian: Unlock Ignite & Transform
Your Language Skills with Contemporary Romance - Book 4
Short Stories in English/Italian: Unlock Ignite & Transform
Your Language Skills with Contemporary Romance - Book 5
Short Stories in English/Italian: Unlock Ignite & Transform
Your Language Skills with Contemporary Romance - Book 6
Short Stories in English/Italian: Unlock Ignite & Transform
Your Language Skills with Contemporary Romance - Book 7
Short Stories in English/Italian: Unlock Ignite & Transform
Your Language Skills with Contemporary Romance - Book 8
Short Stories in English/Italian: Unlock Ignite & Transform
Your Language Skills with Contemporary Romance - Book 9
Short Stories in English/Italian: Unlock Ignite & Transform
Your Language Skills with Contemporary Romance -
Book 10

I Don't Care
If You Don't Like
Me:
I LOVE ME

Preface

Books by Laura Mariani

Introduction

1: I don't care if you don't like me: I LOVE ME

2: The "Inner-Critic" fast

3: Social media fast

4: Know Thyself

5: No, actually ...

6: I AM what I say I AM

7: Mirror Mirror on the wall

8: F***, I start with ME

9: Your bed is your friend

10: A request to your subconscious mind

11: Ooooommm

12: Taller than the trees

13: The mind-body connection

14: Tap into Love

15: R&R

16: Fun is a priority

17: Laugh Out Loud

18: I am grateful for ...

19: What is love?

20: How do I love Thee ...

21: What is your language?

22: Meet the love of your life

23: Flowers feed the soul 24:

The importance of rituals 25:

Be your Valentine

26: Lust is where is at

27: Commit to you

28: Pay it forward

From now on

Get your FREE Ebook

About the Author

Author's Note

Bibliography

Preface

Hello and welcome to **"I Don't Care If You Don't Like Me: I LOVE ME - 28 Ways to Love Yourself More",** - a self-love book with guided practices for women to inspire and enable a journey of self-discovery and self-love.

Here, you will find 28 quick and easy ways to love yourself more every day with techniques you can try and then adopt going forward. Day by day, all these little practices stack up and compound, creating a domino effect, not visible at the beginning but with a massive impact as you move along.

My intention is to support you in loving yourself rotten and feeling like the Goddess that you really are in the process.

And then, just like that, everything in your life

WILL change ...

With love.

Laura xxx

28 Ways To Love Yourself More

Introduction

"How do I love thee? Let Me Count the Ways" is a poem by Elizabeth Barret Browning from the collection "Sonnets from the Portuguese," first published in 1850. Browning dedicated the poem, her most famous and reproduced in endless anthologies of love poetry, to her husband, Robert Browning.

Besides being an exquisite sonnet, most notably here, it is an excellent example of how we can show and feel love for someone.

Likewise, wouldn't it be great if we did the same for ourselves?

Self-love is a habit - **continuously** choosing to think, say, and do what is in your best interest.

We are talking about unconditional, emotional, deep love and passion.

The-I-love-you-no-matter-what which we do naturally for partners and children. It's not that we don't see their faults (common, we do). However, they are irrelevant and don't affect our love.

Isn't it time we did the same for ourselves?

Here are 28 ways to help you do just that.

1: I don't care if you don't like me: I LOVE ME

Some time ago, I saw a video on YouTube with a little girl holding a cup of coffee and, looking straight at the camera, saying:

"*I don't care if you don't like me; I LOVE ME!*" with a nice wink at the end.

Besides thinking the little girl was adorable, I felt she nailed it.
So young but so wise – she intuitively knew what we seem to have forgotten (or forsaken/ignored): the relationship we have with ourselves ultimately defines all of our relationships.

There will always be someone somewhere that doesn't like us.

And you know what? Who cares!!!

So, the first way to love yourself more is to stop relying on external validation and basing the love you have and show yourself on other people's opinions of you.

STOP IT!

And now, repeat after me:

"I don't care if you don't like me; **I LOVE ME**" (with attitude ...)

List any and all sources of external validation you are currently relying on

_____

_____

_____

_____

_____

_____

_____

_____

_____

_____

_____

_____

_____

_____

_____

_____

Write down ten times - "I don't care if you don't like me: I LOVE ME!"

_____

_____

_____

_____

_____

_____

_____

_____

_____

_____

_____

_____

_____

_____

_____

2: The "Inner-Critic" fast

How others treat you (in your professional and personal life) depends on how you project yourself. And **THAT** totally relies on how you view and feel about yourself (and them regarding you).

The famous Inner Critic is alive and kicking. Of course, you would have hoped she could give us a break during these uncertain times. Still, nope...

Considering She (I think of my Inner Critic as a bitchy, jealous, and overly cautious evil twin sister) is not going to stop talking, I don't know about you, but I intend to stop listening.

So, the second way to love yourself more is to practice an "Inner Critic" fast,
AKA:

- Every time the voice in your head suggests something negative, unleash your Inner Child and "**LA LA LA**" back (I know, it sounds very mature, but hey, it's all about what works).

Abstain from listening, and whenever a negative thought crosses your mind:
STOP IT and tell it where to go.

And keep doing so until the voice in your head quotes down ...

Letting Go
Self Criticism

Critical Thought

"I should..."
"I can't believe..."
"I wish..."
"I'm so stupid"

What triggered this thought?

"I was late to the meeting"
"I forgot to call my mom"
"My friend stood me up"

Physical and Emotional Sensations

How does this thought
make you feel?

Compassionate Thought

What you might say if a
friend expressed this
thought

A year from now

How will you feel about
this event next year?
Will it matter?

Concrete Plan

What action can you
take to prepare for
this in future.

Big picture plan

Imagine a future free
from this thought.
What will you do?

Body Scan

Today's Date _____ Time _____

Where are you? _____

Head and Face

Neck and Shoulders

Spine

Hips and Pelvis

Chest

Stomach

Arms

Legs

Whole body sensations

Sensations

Warm - Cold - Soft - Hard -Breeze - Damp - Dry

Tense - Strong - Taut - Numb - Tingling - Tickling - Muscle - Slender - Fragile

Pressure - Throbbing - Blocked - Pulse - Stabbing - Quivering

Nauseous - Shaking - Aching - Breathless - Wired - Anxious

Soothed - Relaxed - Comfortable - Free Flowing

3: Social media fast

The average person spends almost 2 hours per day looking at their favorite social media sites and apps.

This time spent on social media does not support or enable good mental health and self-esteem—less than less self-love.

The continuous comparison with the "greener grass" erodes, slowly but surely, contentment and appreciation for what is good in our lives.

We all need a break from having our lives judged and commented on, often by strangers who don't count.

Detaching from social media is beneficial and recommended.

I have done social media detox several times, one very recently, and it changed my life for the better. My productivity, attention span, and clarity increased significantly. I broke terrible habits (refreshing feeds and checking notifications). And most importantly, I felt freer and happier without social media dictating my life.

And we are now on a quest to love ourselves more, aren't we?

Perfect activity, then ...

4: Know Thyself

Loving yourself more needs, besides silencing your Inner Critic, also being authentic to yourself. This requires knowing your True Self in the first place.

Discovering your true nature and matching how you live to this nature leads to peace of mind and happiness.

And with that comes self-acceptance and belief – when you are true to yourself, everything flows.

So challenge yourself, try some soul searching, and discover more about yourself: what you want (REALLY want), what you like, and what you stand for.

The key word here is YOU, not trying to conform to others' expectations of you.

A great tool you can use is **freewriting**.

Freewriting is simply outpouring streams of consciousness on a page (or more), giving you unrestricted access to your Inner True Self, which can be used to discover more about yourself.

It is a means to an end with neither a right nor a wrong way of doing it.

Write anything and everything that comes to mind.

What do you want, really REALLY want?

_____

_____

_____

_____

_____

_____

_____

_____

_____

_____

_____

_____

_____

_____

_____

_____

Who are YOU?

5: No, actually ...

Another way to stop your Inner Critic from bitching and love yourself more is to substitute negative thinking with Positive Aspects (your positive aspects), AKA:

- Write one positive thing about yourself for every negative thought that comes to mind.

For example, your Bitchy Inner Critic is nagging in your head about not being pretty enough (or as pretty as ...). When it comes up, just say:

"No, actually, I have great eyes (amazing smile, etc., etc.)."

Substitute the criticism with a counter-argument emphasizing a part or more of yourself that you like so that it will ring through to your rational mind.

If you can't find nice things to say about yourself:

1. you are not trying hard enough – there are tons;
2. think about compliments that people give you and positive feedback at work (depending on the negative thought)...

The secret is to have a list of things ready for when your Inner Critic strikes.

Do write down **S-O-M-E-T-H-I-N-G** nice about yourself. NOW!

List all the negative thoughts about yourself
that normally go through your mind

_____

_____

_____

_____

_____

_____

_____

_____

_____

_____

_____

_____

_____

_____

_____

_____

For each negative thought, counter-act with a
"No, actually ..."

_____

_____

_____

_____

_____

_____

_____

_____

_____

_____

_____

_____

_____

_____

_____

_____

6: I AM what I say I AM

The Inner Critic always talks and puts doubts in your mind. The only way to move away from negative thoughts is to replace them with positive ones.

Earl Nightingale said that whatever we plant in our subconscious mind with repetition and emotion will become a reality.

Affirmations are a proven method to prime your brain for positive change. There are different schools of thought on this: some people write them down, and some recite them out loud.

I do both: write them down in my journal – morning and evening – and say them out loud throughout the day.

Two ways of doing them:

1. The so-called **Jackhammer approach:** one positive affirmation said over and over every day,
   a. "hammer" it into your consciousness.
2. The **Hummingbird Approach:** The affirmation changes daily depending on how you feel and what you need during the day.

I use both methods: I have one or two chosen affirmations for something important to me right now that I want to prime my brain fast, and then I have other affirmations that I say scattered throughout the day as needed.

The **Jackhammer approach**, however, is my favorite because it naturally aligns with how the brain learns: by repetition. So, by saying the same thing over and over and over again, firstly, you stop negative thoughts (your brain cannot think two thoughts simultaneously), and secondly, you learn the belief you're trying to acquire.

Let's suppose you are struggling to come up with affirmations. In that case, you can write down all the compliments you have received, the positive feedback from your colleagues, boss, or customers (or teachers), and all the qualities and things you like/love about yourself. Then, turn those phrases into positive affirmations.

For example, from "My boss always tells me my performance exceeds expectations" to "I am great at my job, I am amazing at my job" or " I love how great I am at my job and everything I do."

Because these are phrases you have heard from people either in a position of trust or authority, your rational mind would be more inclined to listen and less resistant to them.

Write a few affirmations applicable to where you are right now in your self-love journey; most importantly, practice telling yourself you ARE those things until they sink in.

You don't have to believe the affirmation; you just need to say them. Over and over and over.

Think about what Muhammad Ali said about beliefs and affirmations:

> *"It's the repetition of affirmations that leads to belief. And once that belief becomes a deep conviction, things begin to happen."*

He talked himself into believing he was the greatest, and then he became so.

Self-love is learned, unfortunately, so we need to practice, practice, and practice some more.

Write down the compliments and positive feedback you normally receive

_____

_____

_____

_____

_____

_____

_____

_____

_____

_____

_____

_____

_____

_____

_____

_____

Turn those compliments/positive feedback into positive "I AM" statements (your affirmations)

_____

_____

_____

_____

_____

_____

_____

_____

_____

_____

_____

_____

_____

_____

_____

_____

_____

_____

7: Mirror Mirror on the wall

Another way to love yourself more is to practice affirmations and positive statements out loud in front of the mirror.

Yes, you read right: in front of the **M-I-R-R-O-R**.

Why is mirror work a great tool?

Because the mirror makes you immediately aware of where you have resistance and the thoughts you need to change, the more uncomfortable you are saying specific affirmations, the more you know you have an issue.

If you don't feel comfortable looking at yourself in the mirror and singing your praises (so to speak), pretend you are paying compliments to your best friend instead of using your affirmations in the first person.

"You look amazing, you are wonderful, etc. …" you get the gist.

You can say your affirmation and/or positive statements each time you are in front of a mirror when you see your reflection or make it part of your daily morning and evening routine.

Or both (PS: try to say them as if you believe them, just saying …. ●).

Your Inner Critic has been talking to you for years, constantly. So, finally, it is time to unleash your Inner Cheerleader.

Practice your affirmations in front of the mirror, and start by using them in the "You are" form - how do you feel?

_____

_____

_____

_____

_____

_____

_____

_____

_____

_____

_____

_____

_____

_____

Now practice them in the "I AM" form - how do you feel now?

_____

_____

_____

_____

_____

_____

_____

_____

_____

_____

_____

_____

_____

_____

_____

_____

_____

8: F***, I start with ME

"F•••, I start with me," said Carrie Fisher in Postcards from the Edge.

Self-care isn't selfish: it's your chance to recharge the batteries (hey, you recharge your mobile phone regularly, right? Well, you need it too) and is one of the steps toward loving yourself every day more.

After all, we take care of the people we love, right? So why not yourself?

Get positive energy flowing and start moving to a place of happiness you might never want to leave. And as soon as you revel in the opportunity to look after yourself, love every bit of yourself, and be by yourself (that's right), you'll be free of loneliness and dependence on external validation.

For me, self-care means meditation, listening to positive talks on YouTube or audiobooks, doing my nails and hair, a face mask, and watching movies that cheer me up (comedy/romance – yep, that's right).

What about you?

What does self-care mean to you?

_____

_____

_____

_____

_____

_____

_____

_____

_____

_____

_____

_____

_____

_____

_____

_____

Self Care Routine

Vision _____

Time	Step

Routine Notes

Food _____

_____

Spiritual _____

_____

Exercise _____

_____

Mantra _____

Daily Tracker

1	2	3	4	5	6	7	8	9	10
11	12	13	14	15	16	17	18	19	20
21	22	23	24	25	26	27	28	29	30
31	Start Date :				End Date :				

9: *Your bed is your friend*

In our quest towards more Self-love, every little thing helps: sleep is one of those things.

Well, actually (good-quality) sleep is more important than people realize, helping to keep you feeling healthy.

Additionally, not sleeping well can make you feel tired and irritable. If this happens regularly, it can significantly affect your health. On the contrary, when you sleep well, you feel refreshed, which helps with de-stressing, concentration, and learning new things.

Most importantly, sleep helps your brain recover and revive itself, allowing the mind to unwind and de-stress. Which, in turn, allows your mental and emotional well-being to be restored.

To help, try to have a bedtime routine:
- Go to bed at a set time

- Remove distractions like your TV, computer, and phone
- Avoid caffeine and alcohol as they can keep you awake (that, unfortunately, includes chocolate)
- Do some relaxing exercises, like yoga
- Stay away from large meals.

What is your current bed routine?

_____

_____

_____

_____

_____

_____

_____

_____

_____

_____

_____

_____

_____

_____

_____

_____

_____

What could you easily implement and stick to it?

_____

_____

_____

_____

_____

_____

_____

_____

_____

_____

_____

_____

_____

_____

_____

10: A request to your subconscious mind

Sleep is an essential part of our lives; it is a crucial part of a self-care routine and, quite frankly, vital for survival.

However, this is not all; sleep can help nourish your self-confidence and love for yourself.

Edison said it: one should only go to sleep after requesting something from the subconscious mind. So why, then, not "request" self-love?

I'm talking here about self-hypnosis. In the same way, you repeat affirmations during the day to replace and counter-act negative thoughts to support your self-love journey; you can listen to affirmations overnight or subliminal messages.

There are countless great videos on YouTube on this subject. Find the one that resonates with you and feeds your mind and your subconscious while sleeping.

You might not remember precisely what is in the video, but you'll see changes in how you think and feel about yourself slowly but surely.

A quick tip:

Suppose you choose a video on YouTube (or any other source/audio) to play overnight. In that case, it is better if the affirmations played are recorded in "you are" statements, as your subconscious mind has a difficult time accepting "I AM" statements from an outside voice or source.

This ensures your affirmations work faster without the need to clear any resistance. You may listen at a low volume with or without earbuds/headphones while you sleep at night.

Alternatively, you could record your own affirmations.

Make a list of affirmation audios that you
could you use to increase your self-love

_____

_____

_____

_____

_____

_____

_____

_____

_____

_____

_____

_____

_____

_____

_____

Listen to them: how do they make you feel?
Choose the one/s the best resonate with you

_____

_____

_____

_____

_____

_____

_____

_____

_____

_____

_____

_____

_____

_____

_____

_____

_____

11: Ooooommm

Various studies have shown how meditation can help relieve stress, manage anxiety, and reduce inflammation.

It also improves memory and concentration.

It's unclear how it confers so many health benefits, but it does.

So here are a few types of meditation practices I have used:

- Focused meditation (concentrating on any of the five senses, like breathing)
- Mantra meditation (uses a repetitive sound to clear the mind). It can be a word, phrase, or sound, such as the famous "Om." It doesn't matter if your mantra is spoken loudly or quietly
- Progressive relaxation (also known as body scan meditation)

- Visualization meditation (imagining joyous scenes or images). Here, it's essential to imagine the scene vividly and use all five senses to add as much detail as possible.

Whichever you choose, ultimately, it's all about what works for you.

You might ask: What does this have to do with loving yourself more?

Meditation quiets the chatter in your mind (the bitchy evil twin sister).

Kind of think of meditation as a form of personal mental hygiene, cleaning all the crap out of your mind.

It also increases self-awareness.
- Done in the morning helps to focus and positively start the day
  - I found the mantra and visualization meditation particularly good in the morning. Perhaps you could use as

your mantra "I LOVE ME" (just a thought ...)?

- Done in the evening helps clear the mind from the day and get ready for a great night's sleep
  - Combined with subliminal affirmations, it's incredible.

Also, remember this:

"Meditation is a way for nourishing and blossoming the divinity within you." - Amit Ray.

And the Divinity within you loves you lots.

All together now: OOOOOOMMMMM ...

12: Taller than the trees

Whether or not you love the outdoors, you must admit that something magical about nature can capture certain emotions.

Being in nature has been proven to make you feel better. It increases self-esteem & decreases depression.

H D Thoreau once said, "*I took a walk in the woods and came out taller than the trees.*"

Going outside in the fresh air is good for us. It encourages physical activity, which gives us positive health benefits. Additionally, it can help develop a sense of ownership and understanding of what our bodies can do rather than what they look like—hopefully, helping us reject an unrealistic ideal set by the media.

We can then, in turn, appreciate our bodies more, leading to a more positive body image and love for self.

Moreover, as the larger ecosystem becomes a more significant issue than waistlines and fashion, nature shifts attention away from self-interest and to more rounded aspects of well-being and the bigger picture.

I love walking outside, especially by the water. I feel the difference in my mood compared to when I'm just working in front of a laptop.

Try it even for 10 minutes: walk in nature (well, outside). I'm sure you'll feel better about yourself afterward.

Take a walk outside for 10 minutes and then come back and write down how you feel?

_____

_____

_____

_____

_____

_____

_____

_____

_____

_____

_____

_____

_____

_____

_____

_____

Schedule quick walking breaks during the day

13: *The mind-body connection*

We have discussed working on the mind because that's where it all starts. The body, however, is essential, too, as we can't go anywhere without it.

Struggling with self-love and, in parallel, with self-image is very common among women (the bitchy twin sister strikes again). The relationship with how we look fluctuates depending on how we feel about ourselves, in a never-ending struggle. Beauty biases are all linked with our emotions about self-esteem, self-image, and how we think about ourselves (back to the mind – the **mind-body connection**).

You know what? It's time to change this!

Instead of fixing everything we think is wrong, let's focus on feeling content with ourselves.

Then, proceed with self-acceptance and self-care, the twins on the journey of self-love.

Caring for ourselves is crucial. Like taking care of our possessions, doing the laundry, and cleaning up the room, we should also remember to care for our bodies, skin, and everything else in between.

Instead of apologizing for our body, we must start apologizing to it. Write a letter and say sorry for all the stupid things we put it through. It stops here.

Enough is enough.

Write yourself a letter and apologize to
yourself and your body for any crap that you
put yourself through

_____

_____

_____

_____

_____

_____

_____

_____

_____

_____

_____

_____

_____

_____

_____

_____

14: Tap into Love

One thing I found to be particularly effective in clearing individual deep-rooted blocks, fears, and insecurities is EFT (Emotional Freedom Technique).

Your subconscious is an aggregation of all your programmed beliefs and emotions related to your appearance/body/self-worth, and love, which has become the absolute truth.

It is not logical, I know. And the more emotional baggage you have, the more likely you will resist losing weight, work on yourself, love yourself, etc.

EFT, better known as Tapping, is one of the most influential and effective mind/body techniques for clearing emotional blocks. There are clinical trials on its efficacy for PTSD, anxiety, and phobias.

EFT uses the fingertips to tap on acupuncture points while emotionally tuning in to negative attitudes and past experiences, allowing people to transform their thoughts and feelings.

You can use EFT tapping to clear fears and blocks towards self-love (or anything really). Additionally, you can also use EFT to tap into your positive affirmations and, by doing so, reinforce them.

Many great practitioners, like *David Childerley, Margaret Lynch Raniere, Brad Yates, and Robert Smith, can show you how to tap with FAST EFT tapping.

*I am not an affiliate of any of these practitioners. I just like their work and use them myself.

Check out some EFT practitioners on YouTube and see who resonates best with you

Put together a compilation of videos that suit
your needs

_____

_____

_____

_____

_____

_____

_____

_____

_____

_____

_____

_____

_____

_____

_____

_____

15: R&R

Relaxing, even for just 5 minutes, can recharge us and give us the energy we need to tackle almost anything; some stress is necessary. However, too much and for too long can be damaging.

Stress can affect our physical, mental, and emotional well-being. Some pressure is necessary. However, too much and too long can be damaging and affect our mental state and emotional state.

And this can exacerbate all those thoughts running wild in our heads.

We can't avoid stress, but we can learn to manage it. Relaxation is one of the keys to managing stress.

When we relax, we have more energy and are calmer, clearer, and more positive overall. This, in turn, helps with feeling better about ourselves being our best Selves and loving ourselves more.

Look after yourself: rest, relax, recharge, and remember to have some fun, too ●.

Finger Labyrinth

Use your finger to slowly trace a path to the center of the labyrinth

Breathe calmly and slowly as you focus.
When you reach the center, draw a long deep breath or two.

Then trace your path back to the outside
Repeat until you feel more focused and calm.

Focus Words

Breathe - Peace - Relax - Tranquility - Serenity - Calm - Space - Beauty
Love - Wonder - Kindness - Light - Happiness - Joy - Warmth

Observations

16: Fun is a priority

Having fun is not frivolous or unproductive. On the contrary, taking time for yourself and the things you enjoy helps build your strength and boost your immune system.

And having fun is good for you!

Well-being balances physical, social, economic, spiritual, and mental aspects. Unique to you. So it is essential to **make room for fun**, irrespective of life priorities.

"*Rule N1: life is supposed to be fun*" – John McGrail.

And having fun helps with feeling better about yourself—another step forward for self-love.

Plan some fun activities

17: Laugh Out Loud

Loving yourself also means accepting yourself and being unapologetically You, no matter what. Even more so being able to laugh at yourself, with yourself.

It is not only good.

It is necessary.

With all your shortcomings, without humiliation, judgment, fear, or self-consciousness.

Believe it or not, laughing out loud, alone, positively affects mood and energy and is amazingly effective. It builds a positive relationship with you because it connects you with, guess?

To you!

And so, when was the last time you had a good laugh? Out loud?

Please go on, do it; you know you want to ●

Practice laughing out loud for no reason

How did you feel about it?

_____

_____

_____

_____

_____

_____

_____

_____

_____

_____

_____

_____

_____

_____

_____

18: I am grateful for ...

Gratitude is the most crucial well-being activity that increases positive emotions, stress hormones, anxiety, and loneliness, even during turbulent times.

Our brain has a negativity bias; our in-built survival mechanism residual from living in caves when staying alive depended on recognizing dangers and running.

We haven't changed that much and still follow the same pattern.

However, this doesn't serve us, in general, and even less when practicing self-love.

There is an abundance of small, seemingly insignificant things to be grateful for – whether it is physical attributes or behaviors, knowledge, or skills, even if it is just being alive instead of looking only for the big-ticket items and waiting to be perfect before we are thankful and celebrate (*perfectionitis* is a terrible disease).

We should appreciate the small things and not let them slip away from sight.
Stack them. Daily.

> "*The More You Express Gratitude For What You Have,*
> *The More Likely You Will Have More To Express Gratitude For*" – Zig Ziglar

And if you note them down, it could make all the difference in how you feel about yourself.

Write down everything your are greatful for about yourself: write every little things and the big things

_____

_____

_____

_____

_____

_____

_____

_____

_____

_____

_____

_____

_____

_____

_____

_____

Keep writing - I know there's more
to write - You are amazing!

19: What is love?

Self-love is a very used expression, and so far, we have touched on different ways to love ourselves more.

To know how to love ourselves truly deeply, we first need to define what love is FOR us. What makes us feel loved.

What is love for you? What does it mean to be truly loved?

Step back and figure out what you need, want, and what makes you feel loved and cherished.

What are your deep-seated needs?

Once you realize what love is to you, well, you are on your way.

What is love for you? What do you need and want?

_____

_____

_____

_____

_____

_____

_____

_____

_____

_____

_____

_____

_____

_____

_____

_____

_____

20: How do I love Thee ...

The phrase "Know thyself" works on the premise that knowledge is inherent. As wisdom is learning to recollect, knowing oneself can be achieved via internal dialogue and introspection.

But what has this got to do with self-love?

If we understand the internal language patterns, we know how to better "communicate and receive love," not just with/toward other people but to ourselves.

Consequently, we can then adapt our communication style to suit the specific audience and occasion to
1. recognize other people's language patterns;
   a. understand what they are trying to say to you;
2. communicate and make people feel loved, and

3. realize how you speak/give and receive love.

State	Primary Sense	Language Pattern
Visual	Sight	I see; it looks good
Audial	Hearing	Sounds good
Kinaesthetic	Feeling	That doesn't feel right

And for your self-love practice, using the right vehicle (audio, visual, or emotional) would go a long, long way ...

Simple, non?

What is your communication style? Are you visual, audial or kinaesthetic?

_____

_____

_____

_____

_____

_____

_____

_____

_____

_____

_____

_____

_____

_____

What is the right vehicle for your self-love practices?

_____

_____

_____

_____

_____

_____

_____

_____

_____

_____

_____

_____

_____

_____

_____

_____

_____

21: What is your language?

Love is a language, and you (me, everybody) need to understand how we communicate in this language.

Think about it: it's the same way as speaking any language. If you are trying to communicate with someone who doesn't speak English, for example, speaking very S-L-O-W-L-Y and very -L-O-U-D-L-Y is not really going to make a difference.

Ditto with communicating love.

Let me give you another example.

When you first fall in love with someone, you use the full spectrum of possibilities; you are trying to have the other person love you back after all. You tell them, show them, touch them, and so on.

But after you are in the stable relationship you wanted, slowly, you (me, everybody) revert to your way of showing love (which ultimately is how you receive love).

It is not that you do not love the person anymore or any less; you have simply reverted to what's comfortable. After all, it can be exhausting talking continuously in another language if it is not innate.

For you, you are showing lots of love. Your partner, on the other hand, might not be "feeling it." Or vice-versa. The phrase "you don't bring flowers anymore" comes to mind.

So, after having identified how you communicate, it is now time to understand your love language.

The different types of languages to express love are:

- words of affirmation,
- quality time,
- physical touch,
- acts of service,
- and receiving gifts.

Knowing your partner's love language is a way to help them feel loved and appreciated throughout the relationship, not just at the beginning.

Ditto with yourself.

Knowing your love language will allow you to build your self-love practices around what is more effective FOR you, not what is fashionable or what some guru has said (including me ●).

What do I mean by this?

Well, if you know, for example, that you like to hear the words I love you or words of appreciation, then when it comes to your morning or evening routine, you might want to use affirmations. Both you affirming out aloud and listening to affirmations on tape/audio.

If you, on the other hand, feel loved by receiving gifts, then make sure you regularly show yourself some love with little (or big) gifts – a candle, flowers, whatever you like.

Speak your language of love to yourself.

Use it as either a habit or **positive reinforcement,** or both.

But use it to your advantage.

What is your love language?

Based on your love language, what are the
self-love practices more effective FOR you?

22: Meet the love of your life

Before we start talking, take a long, deep breath and get your romantic bearing.

Not to find a companion/partner (although this can be extremely useful) or improve a current relationship (ditto) but for yourself.

But to please yourself – that's right - and focus on wrapping yourself in a delicious, warm, cuddly cocoon to transform into the Best You possible and learn to love yourself – truly, deeply, and madly.

Oscar Wilde said, "*Never love anyone who treats you like you're ordinary.*"

Never forget it, and, most importantly, never do it to yourself.

You are special – treat yourself that way, like the Greatest Love you'll ever have.

You are an Amazing Woman. Today, tomorrow, and always.

23: Flowers feed the soul

To love yourself more every day, you need to feed your mind, body, and, most importantly, your soul. And flowers can help with this.

I love roses, any color. And sunflowers.

What about you? What is the flower that makes you smile with joy?

Go and buy yourself some flowers. Just for you. For no reason but to show love to yourself and feed your soul.

If you don't like flowers, do something else.

The point here is to feed your soul, spoil yourself, and enjoy the moment.

It's time to start treating yourself like a Goddess, a Queen.

What are your favorite flowers?

_____

_____

_____

_____

_____

_____

_____

_____

_____

_____

_____

_____

_____

_____

_____

_____

_____

What else feeds your soul and makes you feel special?

_____

_____

_____

_____

_____

_____

_____

_____

_____

_____

_____

_____

_____

_____

_____

_____

24: The importance of rituals

Self-love may mean different things to different people. And it can be elusive.

Sometimes Self-love (loving yourself) is confused with Self-care. Self-care can be one way to show love to yourself, but Self-love is different.

For me, it simply means being my best friend, my own cheerleader, and enjoying being in my own company.

I make a ritual of taking time with me, whether for an hour, a day, a weekend, or longer.

And that includes enjoying going to movies alone, at a park, or reading.

I make it some kind of ceremony that takes me to a special place for me as soon as I start it.

Mentally.

Physically.

Spiritually.

What is your favorite ritual that makes you feel special?

_____

_____

_____

_____

_____

_____

_____

_____

_____

_____

_____

_____

_____

_____

_____

If you don't have one, it's time to choose and plan one

_____

_____

_____

_____

_____

_____

_____

_____

_____

_____

_____

_____

_____

_____

_____

_____

_____

25: Be your Valentine

Be your own Valentine any time of the year.

Take yourself out on a date.

This is a chance to get back in touch with your Inner Self and completely forget about anything or anybody else, at least for your date night.

As you would for any date, put your best foot forward and dress up: you are going out with someone really special, after all.

And as with any long-term relationship, make a habit of having a date night with yourself.

Plan a date with the love your life: YOU

_____

_____

_____

_____

_____

_____

_____

_____

_____

_____

_____

_____

_____

_____

_____

_____

_____

_____

26: Lust is where is at

The relationship with yourself is the longest and most intimate you will ever have.

Self-lust is a part of Self-Love and is necessary for a thriving relationship with you and, somehow, intertwined.

The idea is to recognize and appreciate your sexuality and worthiness. I am not talking about being narcissistic and obsessing over an idealized image.

When you can look at yourself in the mirror and find yourself attractive, the channels of self-confidence and aliveness open.

Being in touch with your sexual magnetism and sexual energy is vital because sexuality is humanity's most profound, primal form of self-exploration and self-expression.

Stand in front of the mirror naked. That's it!

27: Commit to you

So far, we have covered several different practices to love yourself more.

You know what?

They mean nothing unless you actually practice them to start with. And most importantly, if you don't practice them regularly.

You don't go to the gym, do whatever class (really no clue here), and expect to have the best-toned body you have ever had the day after.

Ditto with your mind; you must keep taking that puppy outside whenever it starts playing up with you.

Choose whatever practice (one or more, or all) you have read in this book that you enjoyed or resonated with, and then stick to it.

Make a commitment to yourself and time with you; loving yourself is the best investment you can make.

You are almost at the end of the book: what practices resonate more with you? Which ones didn't?

_____

_____

_____

_____

_____

_____

_____

_____

_____

_____

_____

_____

_____

_____

_____

_____

_____

Make a committment to yourself and plan into your routine/s the practices you liked best

_____

_____

_____

_____

_____

_____

_____

_____

_____

_____

_____

_____

_____

_____

_____

_____

28: Pay it forward

When you can look at yourself in the mirror and find yourself attractive, the channels of self-confidence and aliveness open, and the more secure and self-assured you feel, the more you will notice beauty and qualities in others (women).

As a result, there's no need for competition or comparison.

Don't forget that other women might be going through the same journey toward self-love, and they might not be where you are right now.

In any event, celebrate being a woman and loving yourself, and then pay it forward.

No jealousy. No bitchiness. Just women celebrating and being kind to other women.

And you'll then discover you are in a never-ending cycle of appreciation and enjoyment.

What you give out comes back multiplied.

Celebrate everything wonderful about being a woman and loving yourself

Choose ten women to pay it forward to

From now on

You have made it through the book; thanks for reading it all!

Now it's when the real work begins; if you quit now, you will miss the best part, the real adventure and best relationship you could ever have.

However, for this, you need to have habits that support you and enable you to live your best life, in good or bad times.

Life will throw you curve balls all the time. Unexpected events, situations, and people. Sometimes good and sometimes not so good. And that's why we need to have habits that support us to love ourselves and live our best life.

We are what we think and habitually do.

Think about it: you wake up, have a shower, brush your teeth, and have breakfast or coffee/tea. You have a routine. You don't wake up and start asking: oh my God, what shall I do now? What do I do first? Etc. Etc.

Nope.

You are on autopilot.

Your brain is already trained and drives your activities.

The point here is to create a routine/habits that can and will support you to love yourself, even when unexpected events happen. They will keep you grounded and stable and provide safety and security in the chaos you might be experiencing, so you don't have to "be strong," but you can just be.

Habits to enhance self-care and self-love so when people around you are not exactly kind to you, you still feel cared for and loved. Your brain will take over and remind you that you ARE cared for and loved because you habitually think and act that way. And the same can be said for anything else.

All you seek is inside of you. Create practices that allow for it to come out habitually.

I created the **"28 Days To Love Yourself More Journal with Prompts** - to enable you to take control of your self-love journey and make self-love a habit.

The important thing, irrespective of using my journal or not, is to MAKE self-love a sustainable **HABIT**.

Do what works for you, whatever it is, but do it.

Self-love is a continuous connection with yourself.

Every day.

No matter what.

This requires self-discipline. Not as a punishment but as an act of self-love, constantly choosing what is in your best interest.

Choose Yourself daily.

Even if sometimes it's a pain. It is worthed. You are worthed.

And whatever happens, remember:

"I don't care if you don't like me; **I LOVE ME**" (with attitude ...).

Get your FREE Ebook

Sign up to Laura Mariani The People Alchemist newsletter for a FREE EBOOK - HEAL YOURSELF: A quick HOW-TO guide to deal with anxiety and stress (Techniques and information to learn how to make stress work FOR you instead of AGAINST you and develop resilience in the process).

You'll be the first to hear about new releases, exclusive offers and content on change & transformation for life, business and career.

To claim your free ebook visit:

https://laura-mariani-author.ck.page/freeebook

About the Author

Laura Mariani is a bestselling author of non-fiction success books for women and Change & Transformation Expert. She's the brains behind The People Alchemist, a space for women (and anyone else!) to take charge of their careers and lives.

Laura writes uplifting books that combine positive psychology motivation with a healthy dose of practical tips to help every woman tap into their inner alchemist, changing their lives, businesses, or careers – a bit like magic. Her mission? To Unlock, Ignite, Transform, and, why not, inspire and entertain.

Passionate about smashing barriers, Laura's seen too many talented women miss out on opportunities. It's not that the chances aren't there; it's often about how we approach things. Let's break those limiting beliefs together and rewrite the story.

She is a Change and Transformation expert, Fellow of the Chartered Institute of Personnel & Development (FCIPD), Fellow of the Australian Human Resources Institute (FAHRI), Fellow of the Institute of Leadership & Management (FInstLM), Member of the Society of Human Resources Management (SHRM) and Member of the Change Institute.

You can also follow her on
X (Twitter): x.com/PeopleAlchemist
Instagram: instagram.com/lauramariani_author
LinkedIn: linkedin.com/in/lauramariani-fcipd

Author's Note

Thank you so much for buying "**I Don't Care if You Don't Like Me: I LOVE ME - 28 Ways to Love Yourself More**" - a self-love book with guided practices.

I hope you enjoyed it. A review would be much appreciated as it helps other readers to discover these practices and book. Thanks.

Bibliography

I read different books as part of my research. Some of them, together with other references, include

A Theory of Human Motivation - **Abraham Maslow**

Love Your Body - **Louise Hay**
Psycho-Cybernetics - **Maxwell Maltz**
Self Mastery Through Conscious Autosuggestion - **Émile Coué**
The Artist Way - **Julia Cameron**
The Complete Reader - **Neville Goddard**, compiled and edited by **David Allen**
The 5 Love Languages by **Gary Chapman**.

David Childerley https://www.davidchilderley.com/
Margaret Lynch Raniere
https://members.margaretlynchraniere.com/

Robert Smith https://www.fastereft.com/

Brad Yates https://www.tapwithbrad.com/

Printed in Great Britain
by Amazon

36946001R00076